Luigi Boccherini

Quintet for Guitar and String Quartet

No. 4 in D major, G448

"Fandango"

3601

LUIGI BOCCHERINI
Quintet for Guitar and Strings In D Major

(G.448)

(1743–1805)

I

Guitar

II

Guitar

Allegro maestoso

Guitar

[poco cresc.]

III

Grave assai

dolce

[poco] cresc.

[pp]

[f]

Fandango

a) Orig.

MMO MUSIC GROUP, INC., 50 Executive Boulevard, Elmsford, NY 10523-1325